7 PRINCIPLES OF COMMONWEALTH LEADERSHIP

ANDRE THOMAS

GREATNESS PUBLISHING

www.12slm.org

Published by Greatness Publishing, Ontario, Canada

Cover design and formatting by Farouk Roberts

Library and Archives Canada
ISBN 978-1-927579-20-6

All Scripture quotations are from the King James Version of the Bible, except otherwise stated.

www.greatnesspublishing.com

This workbook is for use with the 12 Spheres of Leadership Movement program.

DEDICATION

To the members of Divine Visitation Assemblies:

You are a city set on a hill and your greatness will not be hidden

ACKNOWLEDGMENTS

Thanks to Farouk Roberts for his graphic design, and Natalie M. Ali for her help in typing out this manuscript.

Cathy-Ann Forde for proofreading for editing

Last but not least I praise the Lord Jesus Christ for entrusting me with the revelation of the 12 Spheres of Leadership and how they impact the destinies of nations.

TABLE OF CONTENTS

CHAPTER ONE

GOD IS THE CREATOR AND MODEL OF LEADERSHIP

Principle: God is the creator and greatest model of leadership and teamwork.

The Heavenly Father as Leader

The God that created us is a leader and the creator of leadership. He exists within a team of the God the Father, God the Son and God the Holy Ghost of which the Father is the visionary. The Bible tells us that in the beginning God created the Heavens and the Earth. This same scripture can be paraphrased this way: In the beginning, God the Father had a vision to create the heavens and the earth, and He uses His influence with God the Son and God the Holy Spirit to create His masterpiece.

In the book of Genesis 1:26, the phrase "Let us" is the language of leadership and teamwork. It is the voice of a leader asking His team, to work together with Him to bring His vision to fulfillment.

<u>What is Leadership?</u>

- Leadership is working through and with people to fulfill a vision.

- Leadership is shaping the future with ideas and working through people to turn the ideas into reality.

- Leadership is the application of the influencing of people to fulfill a vision.

- The human spirit contains gifts from God while the soul contains passion and competence. Leaders have ideas on how the future should be and they use various methods of influence to unlock the innate gifting, passion and competence of people to take their ideas from concept to reality.

- Leadership is required when a vision requires the participation of more than one person for its fulfillment.

The Godhead functions in a team - God the Son and God the Holy Spirit work together to bring the vision of God the Father to fulfillment.

<u>What is Vision?</u>

- Vision is the birthplace of leadership. It is the fountain that produces the need of leadership. It is a clear mental portrait of a preferred future.

The Heavenly Father had a vision for the heavens and the earth that was not yet created.

- God the Father also had a vision and idea to create man. Man existed in the womb of God's thinking, and He worked with God the Son and God the Holy Spirit to bring man out of the womb of His thinking into reality.

- Man was made in the image and likeness of God. The word 'image' means external representation and the word 'likeness' means internal qualities. Man was made to look like God on the outside, and have God's qualities on the inside.

- God is a creative visionary leader who partners and works with other beings like himself. He partnered with God the Son and God the Holy Spirit to take His vision from concept to reality. This portrait of God as a creative visionary is evident from the book of Genesis where the story of creation unfolds.

- You were also made to carry out vision through teamwork, as you were made in the image and likeness of God. Therefore, you have within you the capacity to function as a creative visionary leader in the sphere of your gifting, and the ability to work with other people to bring your visions and ideas from concept to reality.

You are a leader because you were made in the image and likeness of a leader.

Write out an example of a vision that you are passionate about that requires the participation of other people for its fulfillment.

_____

_____

_____

The Heavenly Father as Team Leader and Team Builder

- The Heavenly Father leads the Godhead team that is made of Himself, God the Son and God the Holy Spirit.

Mat 28:19 "Go therefore and make disciples of all the nations, baptizing them in the name of the Father and of the Son and of the Holy Spirit."

- The Heavenly Father created the Angelic Team and work through them to accomplish His will in the universe.

Rev 5:11 "Then I looked, and I heard the voice of many angels around the throne, the living creatures, and the elders; and the number of them was ten thousand times ten thousand, and thousands of thousands."

Team God and Adam

- God brought the animals to Adam and asked him to name them when he could have done it himself. He chose to work with Adam as a team member.

- God's plan is still the same. He desires to work in partnership with mankind, with man's role as the junior partner and Him in the leading role as the senior partner.

Gen 2:19 Out of the ground the LORD God formed every beast of the field and every bird of the air, and brought them to Adam to see what he would call them. And whatever Adam called each living creature that was its name.

The Marriage Team

God then created the Marriage team because he did not want Adam to be without a human team member.

Gen 2:21-22 And the LORD God caused a deep sleep to fall on Adam, and he slept; and He took one of his ribs, and closed up the flesh in its place. Then the rib which the LORD God had taken from man, He made into a woman, and He brought her to the man.

- The greatest revelation of marriage is that its partners (male and female) were designed by God to function as a team, and if the principles of teamwork are not adhered to, the end result will be a fracture in the partnership.

Jesus: The Leader and Team Builder

Jesus Christ began His earthly missionary by taking a leadership approach. He was not a one-man spiritual Holy Ghost Rambo. He functioned as a leader of an organization that had several distinctive teams.

The Executive Team

Mat 10:1 And when He had called His twelve disciples to [Him], He gave them power [over] unclean spirits, to cast them out, and to heal all kinds of sickness and all kinds of disease.

This team of 12 was His executive team and He worked with and through them to accomplish His purposes on earth.

The Outreach Team

- Jesus then had an outreach team made up of 70 disciples and He worked with them and through them to take His anointing and message to the cities of Israel.

Luke 10:1 After these things the Lord appointed seventy others also, and sent them two by two before His face into every city and place where He Himself was about to go.

Financial Partnership Team

- Jesus also had a third team which was a financial partnership team made up of women, who the scriptures said provided for Him from their substance.

Luke 8:1 Now it came to pass, afterward, that He went through every city and village, preaching and bringing the glad tidings of the kingdom of God. And the twelve were with Him, and certain women who had been healed of evil spirits and infirmities-- Mary called Magdalene, out of whom had come seven demons, and Joanna the wife of Chuza, Herod's steward, and Susanna, and many others who provided for Him from their substance.

Holy Spirit: The Leader and Builder

- The Holy Spirit worked in a team with Jesus during His earthly ministry.

Act 1:2 Until the day in which He was taken up, after He through the Holy Spirit had given commandments to the apostles whom He had chosen.

- The Holy Spirit works as the leader and senior partner in teamwork with the servants of the Lord.

Act 13:1 Now in the church that was at Antioch there were certain prophets and teachers: Barnabas, Simeon who was called Niger, Lucius of Cyrene, Manaen who had been brought up with Herod the tetrarch, and Saul. As they ministered to the Lord and fasted, the Holy Spirit said, "Now separate to Me Barnabas and Saul for the work to which I have called them." Then, having fasted and prayed and laid hands on them, they sent [them] away. So, being sent out by the Holy Spirit, they went down to Seleucia, and from there they sailed to Cyprus.

- In a study of the scriptures, the Holy Spirit asked the leaders of the Antioch church to separate Barnabas and Paul for the work to which He had called them. This is teamwork. The Holy Spirit is still working with the servants and the handmaidens of the Lord in holy partnership with Him in this time.

CHAPTER TWO
LEADERSHIP AND TEAMWORK

Principle: Leadership and teamwork is required if the execution of a vision requires the participation of more than one individual.

- God creates human teams. God created the team of Adam and Eve to birth the human race.

- God created the team of Abraham and Sarah to birth the nation of Israel.

- God created the team of Moses, Aaron and Marion to take the children of Israel from bondage to the Land of Canaan.

- Jesus sent out the 70 in teams of two to reach the cities of Israel.

- The Holy Spirit created the team of Paul and Barnabas to reach the Gentile world.

Give an example of a marriage, ministry, or project that failed because of the lack of teamwork.

_____
_____
_____
_____
_____

- One is too small a number to achieve anything of significance. There is nothing significant under the sun that has ever been done by one person acting by themselves. Even Batman had Robin to help him. Lone rangers and one-man bands do not see the manifestation of significant visions. If your vision or clear mental portrait of the future is to drink a cup of water in five minutes, you usually do not need leadership or teamwork for its accomplishment.

- However, if your vision is to build a great marriage, build a great family, lead an effective department, build a great church, run a successful business, represent your country at the Olympics or be a world class singer you will have to work with people and through people in a team environment. All effective teams have these particular attributes:

1. Clear vision.

2. Clear goals and strategy on the pathway to fulfill the vision.

3. Clear values that represent the team.

4. Clear roles and responsibilities.

5. Genuine care and concern for welfare of the team.

6. Clear communication that seeks to understand and be understood.

7. An atmosphere of unity and cooperation.

Challenges in Building and leading Teams

One of the greatest teams in the Bible was the executive team consisting of the 12 Apostles of Jesus Christ. This team comprised of the good, the bad and the ugly; in other words, the team had all the characteristics that essentially make up a team.

- The greatest in the team was their partnership with Jesus to reach Israel and birth the church.

- There were good attitudes in the team which were evident when they stayed united despite challenges and different personalities.

- There were bad issues in the team because one of the team members Judas, was a thief, and James and John secretly lobbied for the highest positions in the team.

- There were ugly issues in the team as Judas betrayed the visionary leader of the team with a deceitful kiss and then committed suicide.

- All teams in their raw state will have a combination of the great, the good, the bad and the ugly; however, it takes operating in the wisdom of God to efficiently and effective manage these attributes so that the end result will be a winning team.

- The essence of a great team is that although its leader may have weaknesses, there are no weaknesses in the team as a whole.

CHAPTER THREE
YOUR SPHERE OF INFLUENCE

Principle: The innate gifts that God has given you when developed, creates the room and sphere of your influence.

Prov 18:16: A man's gift makes room for him, and brings him before great men.

The Uncommon Gift in You

An uncommon gift is a divine ability freely given to produce something valuable with the minimum outlay of effort, time or study. Gifts operate in different areas of life such as:

1. Sphere of Spiritual Leadership
2. Sphere of Philosophic Leadership
3. Sphere of Political Leadership
4. Sphere of Entrepreneurial Leadership
5. Sphere of Military & Law Enforcement Leadership
6. Sphere of Educational Leadership
7. Sphere of Social Care Leadership
8. Sphere of Family Leadership
9. Sphere of Judicial Leadership
10. Sphere of Media Leadership
11. Sphere of Arts & Entertainment Leadership
12. Sphere of Organizational Leadership

- Some people uncommon gifts are predominantly in one sphere, such as John the Baptist whose gifts were Prophet and Preacher. He only operated in the Sphere of Spiritual leadership.
- Other people like David whose uncommon gifts were King, Military Commander, Minstrel, and Prophetic Psalmist operated in the spheres of Political, Spiritual and Military and Law Enforcement Leadership.

Jam 1:17: Every good gift and every perfect gift is from above, and comes down from the Father of lights, with whom there is no variation or shadow of turning.

Abuse of God-given Gifts

A good example of the abuse of a God-given gift is seen in the life of the daughter of Herodias, who was one of the great dancers of her generation. Her dance for the king was so captivating and pleasurable that he asked her to name the kingly reward she wanted and it will be granted. She then asked for the head of John the Baptist. While the gift to dance was God-given, the use of the gift was for satanic purposes. She could have asked for the release of John the Baptist and it would have been granted. This story is a prime example of the abuse of influence produced by a God-given gift.

Identifying and Developing the Uncommon Gift in You

- Identifying and developing your uncommon gift, is the key to developing your influence. Very few people inherit influence from their parents, but everybody can become influential, by becoming great at using their gifts to add value to people.

- Nobody is without an uncommon gift; however, the gift in you must be developed to the point that it can significantly add value to people.

- The daughter of Herodias had the gift of dancing which most people would not classify as an outstanding gift. However, when she danced for Herodias it was not the dance of an amateur. It was the dance of a woman who had developed her gift and when her moment came, she maximized it and allowed Satan to use the platform of influence it created.

- Influence by design works in the following ways:

  1. The daughter of Herodias had influence, because she had developed her dancing skills, which she used to add value to the King and put a smile on his face.

  2. She then leveraged the influence that the gift created and asked for the head of John the Baptist.

- This example was used to prove that if you develop your gift and serve it with distinction, it will create a sphere of influence and leadership for you in this world.

- Highly developed gifts, regardless of what type they are, when served with excellence, always bring people before great men and women.

CHAPTER FOUR
GOD'S LEADERSHIP IDEOLOGY

Principle: God leads for the commonwealth of those He created.

There are many concepts and philosophies about leadership. Indeed, it is one of the most talked about, researched and debated subjects on the earth. However, the greatest leader of all wrote the greatest book on the subject of leadership; our Heavenly Father, the One whose leadership vision included you and me.

There are different leadership approaches and in my studies I have been able to identify three distinct leadership philosophies.

1.   Commonwealth Leadership Philosophy

- This is the Biblical ideology which is evident in Ephesians 2:12. This type of leadership exercises influence for the common wealth of the group of people it is leading. It shapes the future with ideas so that those under its influence would increase in wealth, progress, breakthroughs, and all things good. It is the type of leadership that was exercised by Moses, Joshua, David, Solomon, Nehemiah, Deborah

Esther and the Apostles Paul and Peter

Joshua led the people of Israel into the Promised Land and he, along with the Israelite army was victorious in conquering the cities of Jericho and Ai. As a result of those common victories, every tribe in Israel was enthusiastic in the quest to pursue and occupy their own territory.

- This type of leadership finds its joy in increasing the quality of life of the people under its care. Its joy is not in the individual gift, influence or wealth of the leader but it is in how the leader uses his gifts, knowledge, and wealth to increase the collective influence, wealth and welfare of the people under its care.

- Commonwealth Leadership focuses on others. It is the way of the servant leader.

2. Emperor Leadership Philosophy

- The Emperor Leadership philosophy states that the people who are under the influence of the leader exist only to create a platform for that leader's ambition. They are mobilized, manipulated if necessary, and forced if required, to sustain, protect and advance the throne of the Emperor. The subjects of that influence are simply what petrol is to a car – human fuel. This type of leadership sees people as expendable with the same value as petrol.

3. Transactional Leadership Philosophy

- Transactional Leadership can be defined as a "quid pro quo" arrangement; i.e., I scratch your back and you in turn scratch mine. If I hired you at a rate of $20 per hour and you complete the tasks assigned, you will be paid the $20. There is no loyalty involved as the performance exhibited within the arrangement is motivated by the value of the transaction. It is this leadership style that governs much of the business world. However, this type of leadership is limited, as the greatest things in the world like loyalty, friendship, love, honor, and dedication cannot be traded. A family, army, city, nation and ground breaking business cannot be led into greatness by employing the philosophy of Transactional Leadership.

Moses: A Commonwealth Leader

- In Exodus 3:19-22, the Lord God told Moses that He will give the Israelites favour in the sight of the Egyptians so that they will not leave Egypt empty-handed. He wanted them to acquire possessions under Moses' leadership. He wanted the leadership of Moses to not only deliver the people, but to profit the people even in its initial stages.
- Almost every person will agree that the Israelites owed a huge debt to Moses because He facilitated their deliverance from slavery. However, the Commonwealth philosophy which Moses used as his mental lens to lead brought the people into profit. This is very different from the ideology of many leaders who say "I don't want the people to profit; I only want myself to profit; the people exist for my profit". A Commonwealth Leader leads for the profit of the people under his influence.

Saul: An Emperor Leader

- In 1 Samuel 14:20-30, 43-45, it was stated that Jonathan partnered with God in his capacity as a Military leader and brought about a victory against the enemies of Israel. He was a game changer. We see that Saul made a stupid oath based on his emotions and not his intellect charging no man to eat food that day, even after fighting. His son Jonathan, unaware of the oath came in after leading a great victory and ate some honey. And his father, upon finding this out in the aftermath of the battle is determined to have him killed because he broke the oath. It is obvious that in the value system of Saul, his son Jonathan, his military champion was expendable. He was simply human fuel to Saul and the gift of gratitude and appreciation for Jonathan's exploits was non-existent.

- That is the characteristic of an Emperor Leader. He/she has no appreciation and loyalty to individuals, even if a person has made a great contribution that has changed the fortunes of the team, city or nation. Everyone is expendable to an Emperor Leader.

Balak: A Transactional Leader

- In Numbers 22-24 Balak, King of Moab, feared that the approaching children of Israel had military might and would overthrow him and seize his territory. He then entered into a transaction with Balaam, which involved paying him a sum of money to prophesy against the children of Israel.

- Balaam and Balak did not share the same values, vision or loyalties. It was simply a transaction. The only influence that Balak had over Balaam was the influence of the money being offered, and the only influence that Balaam had on Balak was the perceived value of what his prophetic gift could bring to Balaam.

a) Name an example of another Commonwealth Leader in the Bible.
b) State the reason for your choice.

_____
_____
_____
_____
_____
_____
_____
_____
_____

_____
_____

a) Name an example of another Transactional Leader in the Bible.
b) State the reason for your choice.

_____
_____
_____
_____
_____
_____
_____
_____
_____
_____

a) Name an example of another Emperor Leader in the Bible.
b) State the reason for your choice.

_____
_____
_____
_____
_____
_____
_____
_____
_____
_____

CHAPTER FIVE

IDEAS AND SOLUTIONS

Principle: The problems of a nation will never be greater than the ideas and solution within people who are sent by God to that nation.

During an experience with God, the voice of the Lord came to me and said "that the problems of a generation will never be greater than the ideas and solutions within people born into that generation, otherwise God has set us up to fail."

I recalled listening to a radio program from World War II where one of the great American Generals was being interviewed about the situation in the world at that time. This was in the era of world leaders like Hitler, Mussolini, Stalin in Europe and the Emperor of Japan in Asia; and the radio program interviewer was in a panic saying "we are going to have to pray to God to move these mountains." This is because these political leaders had genocidal tenancies and they had no hesitation in killing many people to accomplish their purposes. However, that great American General had an insight into how heaven solves problems on the earth and he said "we do not need to pray for God to move the mountains; we need to pray for God to give us men and women who can match and move these mountains."

Let us consider the following:

- If the problems of a nation are greater than the ideas and the solutions within the people sent to that nation, then God has set up that nation to fail.

- There was a flood coming upon the earth to destroy the human race, but on a man called Noah, came a divine idea and solution to build a boat that preserved the human race and animals.

- The children of Israel were in cruel bondage to the super power of Egypt and on a man called Moses, came a divine idea and a solution to bring them out of bondage.

- The children of Israel were stuck in the wilderness and on a young man called Joshua, came a divine idea and solution to take them into the Promise land.

- The soldiers of Israel were frightened and backed into a corner by their opposition; they were led by King Saul, who had lost his divine anointing. These soldiers polished their swords, put on their armor and walked to the battlefield everyday where they were confronted by the giant "Goliath", who asked for a showdown with their champion soldier. Goliath was such a terrifying sight, the soldiers ran back to their tents in fear. The nation was in a crisis, but on a young man called David came a divine idea and solution for the national crisis. He rose up in the power of that solution and defeated the giant.

There are Goliath problems facing the nations of this world and there is no information that can be accessed from history to solve these problems. They are as challenging as Goliath was to Israel.

- There are Social Goliaths in nations where women are the head of up to 70% of households and their male children lack a father figure to mentor them into manhood.

- There are Economic Goliaths facing cities where the major industries that employ the masses have closed, resulting in high unemployment in these areas.

- There are Military Goliaths in the form of terrorism facing nations.

- There are Spiritual Goliaths facing nations as apathy and witchcraft rises.

- There are Moral Goliaths facing nations where young children aged 9 and 10, take guns to school, and 1 in every 6 college students, has an STD.

These problems are not greater than the ideas and solutions within the Davids of that nation. Will you rise and become a David in your nation?

There is a divine idea in you. There is a divine solution inside of you, which you were born to serve. Everything God creates, he makes to contribute to another. These ideas and solutions are within you in the form of an uncommon vision. Your awareness of this truth is the discovery of the greatest version of you.

- You were not born to be a consumer; you were born to be a contributor. You were not born to be a taker; you were born to be a solution.

- When the nation of Israel was facing extinction, God raised up a woman called Esther with a divine idea and solution within her for the problem.

One day God spoke to me while watching a news program on TV. A member of the Red Cross was at the sight of a hurricane in Honduras and he was complaining that there were not enough people volunteering to be rescue workers.

At that moment, God spoke to me and said "the reason for that Andre is that some of those people were aborted. People, who were ordained before the foundation of the world to be rescue workers, were not alive on the earth because they were aborted. However, the greatest tragedy is found in the people who can be characterized as the 'living dead,' that is, people who are alive and are disconnected from their divine idea and solution.

Death in the Bible means disconnection

- Spiritual death is disconnection from God.
- Physical death occurs when your spirit disconnects from your body.
- Destiny death is to be alive but disconnected from the divine ideas you were born to manifest and the divine solution you were born to serve others.

I wrote this workbook to rescue you from Destiny death. Someone needs the solution you carry. God saved you because he loves you, but he calls you to serve a solution because he loves someone else.

Your life must benefit others if you must truly live.

What is your solution? What is the divine idea that God has placed in your heart?

_____

_____

_____

CHAPTER SIX

LEADERSHIP WISDOM

Principle: Except the leadership wisdom in the visionary matches his vision, the vision will bring the visionary frustration.

Ideas and solutions take the form of an uncommon vision which dwells within your spirit. This vision is not borrowed, but was birthed in you. It was formed within you. It looks like God and it looks like you.

- It looks like God because it will take the grace of God for it to be done through you.

- It looks like you because it maximizes the innate gifts, talents, abilities, wisdom, passion and energy that God has placed within you.

- However, for this vision to be done, the wisdom of God within you must match the vision.

What is wisdom?

Wisdom is thinking thoughts and applying principles to create what you desire. In other words, wisdom is creativity in action.

Where wisdom is displayed, creativity naturally follows.

There are four types of wisdom:

1. Common sense, which is thinking common thoughts and applying common principles to create common results.

2. Intellectual wisdom, which is thinking thoughts and applying principles to create notable things for humanity.

3. Demonic wisdom, which is thinking demonic thoughts and applying demonic principles to create hell on earth.

4. Divine wisdom, which is thinking divine thoughts and applying principles to create God's dream and heaven's will on the earth.

The word of God reveals that God by wisdom created the heavens and the earth:

- Prov 3:19 The LORD by wisdom hath founded the earth; by understanding hath He established the heavens.

- Prov 3:20 By His knowledge the depths are broken up, and the clouds drop down the dew.

- Psalm 104:24 O LORD, how manifold are thy works! in wisdom hast thou made them all: the earth is full of thy riches.

Wisdom is what God uses to create. Since mankind was made in the image of God, it stands to reason that we must operate in the wisdom of God in order to see the fulfillment of our God-given visions.

Ecc 10:15 The labour of the foolish wearieth every one of them, because he knoweth not how to go to the city.

If the wisdom of God in you does not match the vision God has given you, the vision God has given you will become the object of your frustration.

There are many people in the Bible that had a vision that was greater than the wisdom and creativity of God in them. Solomon is an excellent example.

1Ch 22:5 And David said, Solomon my son is young and tender, and the house to be built for Jehovah is to be highly magnificent, for a name and for beauty to all the lands. I will now prepare for it. And David prepared abundantly before his death.

What is the Solomon Problem?

David knew that Solomon had received a mandate from God, but did not have the wisdom of God to partner with God and people to take the vision from concept to reality.

The Solomon problem is having a vision that is greater than your wisdom.

2Chr 1:6-12 And there at the bronze altar, Solomon offered a thousand animals as sacrifices to please the LORD. God appeared to Solomon that night in a dream and said, "Solomon, ask for anything you want, and I will give it to you." Solomon answered: LORD God, you were always loyal to my father David, and now you have made me King of Israel. I am supposed to rule these people, but there are as many of them as there are specks of dust on the ground. So keep the promise you made to my father and make me wise. Give me the knowledge I will need to be the king of this great nation of yours. God replied: Solomon, you could have asked me to make you rich or famous or to let you live a long time. Or you could have asked for your enemies to be destroyed. Instead, you asked for wisdom and knowledge to rule my people. So I will make you wise and intelligent. But I will also make you richer and more famous than any king before or after you.

- The solution to Solomon's problem was to ask God for wisdom.

Many people reading this manual have the Solomon's problem. God has given you something to do but you do not know how to do it. The Solomon problem was solved by divine wisdom. Your answer is a baptism in the Wisdom of God. Divine wisdom empowers a person to partner with their design, God, and people to take a vision from concept to reality.

Partnership with God

Many people do not know how to partner with God. The word partnership can be explained as the various parts of a ship working together, going in the same direction. Many times God and his people are not on the same frequency or going in the same direction. God wants to partner with His people like He did with Adam in the naming of the animals.

Partnership with your design

If you do not love yourself you cannot partner with yourself. If you do not understand yourself and comprehend your gifts, strengths, weaknesses and destiny, you will fight yourself. The greatest civil wars that people fight are the wars fought within them.

Partnership with others

Divine wisdom enables you to identify and locate the men and women you are supposed to partner with to accomplish the purposes of God in your life. No divine purpose is fulfilled without partnership. It took the partnership of God the Son and God the Holy Ghost to make man. It took the partnership of your mom and dad for you to be born and it will take partnership with others for your destiny to be fulfilled. If you cannot successfully partner with people, the fulfillment of your vision and destiny will never be a reality.

CHAPTER SEVEN
THE GREATNESS OF NATIONS

Principle: The greatness of a nation will not emerge except the greatness of its leaders emerges.

Revelation 21:22-26 states "And I saw no temple in it, for the Lord God Almighty is its temple, even the Lamb. And the city had no need of the sun, nor of the moon, that they might shine in it, for the glory of God illuminated it, and its lamp is the Lamb. And the nations of those who are saved will walk in the light of it; and the kings of the earth bring their glory and honor into it. And its gates may not be shut at all by day, for there shall be no night there. And they shall bring the glory and honor of the nations into it."

God has not only given glory and honor to individuals, He has also given them to nations. This Scripture brings to light the following truths:

- In eternity the glory and honor of nations will be celebrated.

- God has put an aspect of Himself called His glory into every nation.

- Every nation has been given a unique honor and value among the other nations.

- The greatness of a nation is its manifested glory and honor.

- If a nation follows God's program, it will have an expression of divinity that will be manifested as unique, divine solutions that can be served to the world.

- The greatness of a nation will not emerge if the greatness of its leaders does not emerge.

- The glory and honor of a nation will never emerge if the glory and honor of its leaders does not emerge.

- Heaven celebrates the manifestation of the glory and honor of leaders and nations.

Different types of leaders must manifest their personal glory and honor for the greatness of a nation to emerge. Your nation, irrespective of the circumstances in which it finds itself, has God-given glory and honor hidden in its destiny. Satan's goal is to block its manifestation.

"I say the truth in Christ, I lie not, my conscience also bearing me witness in the

Holy Ghost, that I have great heaviness and continual sorrow in my heart. For I could wish that I myself were accursed from Christ for my brethren, my kinsmen according to the flesh: Who are Israelites; to whom pertaineth the adoption, and the glory, and the covenants, and the giving of the law, and the service of God, and the promises; Whose are the fathers, and of whom as concerning the flesh Christ came, who is over all, God blessed forever. Amen."

(Romans 9:1-5).

- In studying the evolution of nations, we realize that all nations came from Noah and his three sons Shem, Ham and Japheth (see Genesis 10). Genesis 11 states that all nations spoke the same language and had "one speech," and they decided to build a tower that would reach the heavens. This they determined to do in their own name, not in the name of God, their Creator.

- God saw their plan and stopped the project giving each nation its own language. He then called Abram (Genesis 12) and gave him an assignment to create a model nation. Through this model nation God intended to bless all the other nations of the earth. His dealings with this nation would showcase how He would deal with other nations, and this nation would become a light to all nations.

- In the first few chapters of the book of Exodus, Israel is in bondage as a nation. The Hebrew people were serving Egypt as slaves both physically and economically. However, in the womb of that oppressed nation was its glory and honor.

Israel's glory and honor is identified in Romans 9:4-5. To Israel, belong the adoption, the glory, the covenants, and the service of God, the promises, the fathers and Christ according to the flesh, which can be broken down as follows:

Adoption: The process for being adopted into the family of God was revealed to Israel and through Israel to the world.

The Glory: The nature of the glory of God was revealed to Israel in the events described in the book of Exodus, and through Israel in the ministry of Jesus to the world.

The Covenants: The old and the new covenant were revealed to Israel and through Israel to the world.

The Giving of the Law: The law found in the Old Testament with its rules and regulations was given to Israel and through Israel to the world.

The Service of God: The protocol, process and qualifications for serving God as a priest, king and servant were given to Israel and through Israel to the world.

The Promises: Gods general promises to mankind were revealed to Israel and through Israel to the world.

The Fathers: The fathers of the faith in the Old Testament and the Apostles in the New Testament were all of Israeli descent. Israel shared these men with the world.

The Christ: In His humanity, Jesus was a Jewish man. This was Israel's greatest gift to the world.

These unique gifts to the world are Israel's glory and honor. Just as Israel has glory and honor unique to itself, so has every nation.

Emergence of Israel's Glory and Honor

Satan, through the Pharaoh, a political leader, was restraining Israel's glory and honor from manifesting. That happens to nations governed by ungodly men and women when political and other leaders hold the nation in bondage. But just as God reserved Moses, Aaron and Miriam for the leadership of Israel, so is He reserving leaders in the nations of the world to take these nations from bondage into their God-given destinies. Canada, Germany, Costa Rica, Haiti, Indonesia, Australia, Nigeria, Bulgaria and all other nations of the world, possess God-given glory and honor. You may be ashamed of your nation, or of your leaders, but righteous leadership can uncover and manifest your nation's glory and honor. It is time to contend for the glory and honor of every nation to emerge.

What is the glory and honor of your nation?

_____

_____

OTHER BOOKS BY ANDRE THOMAS

1. The Organizational Visionary
2. The Gift of Political Leadership
3. 12 Spheres of Leadership (The 12 types of leaders that shape the destinies of nations)
4. Unlock Your Greatness (A Young Leaders' Handbook)
5. Discovering Me
6. Uncommon Men and Distinguished Women
7. Coaching People into the 12 Spheres of Leadership
8. Seven Principles of Commonwealth Leadership
9. Discovering your Leadership Assignment
10. Preparing for your Leadership Assignment
11. Executing your Leadership Assignment
12. I Am a Leader (Inspiring Greatness in Kids)
13. The Entrepreneurial Visionary
14. The Social Visionary
15. From Brokenness to Wholeness

ABOUT THE 12 SPHERES OF LEADERSHIP MOVEMENT

Purpose

To raise up a global movement of the 12 types of leaders that shape the destinies of nations.

Our Mission

To influence and empower two million leaders globally to execute divine assignments in the 12 spheres of leadership.

Our Method

<u>Conferences</u>

To form strategic partnerships with key national leaders to hold 12 Spheres of Leadership conferences, events and speaking engagements.

<u>Media and Communication</u>

1. We create media programs and a media platform to distribute 12 Spheres of Leadership Content to the World.
2. We communicate monthly to our partners through 'Leadership Fuel' a monthly audio teaching and news digest.

<u>Books</u>

We write, publish and distribute books that influence and empower leaders globally to execute divine assignments in the 12 spheres of leadership.

How can your church, town, city or nation be transformed by the 12 Spheres of Leadership Movement?
There are 3 different events that Bishop Andre Thomas may be booked for:

1. LEADERSHIP WISDOM EXPLOSION

    An event where:

- The biblical wisdom of the 12 Spheres of Leadership is imparted to equip the saints and to shape the destiny of their nation.

- Visionaries are refreshed by the Holy Spirit.

- This event can also be customized to focus on specific spheres of leadership

2.   ANOINTING REVIVAL

An event where:

- A fresh anointing is imparted to people individually and in mass to unlock their God given greatness.

- The delivering and healing power of God is also administered to set people free from all bondage.

3.   ANOINTING AND WISDOM CONFERENCE

This event features the best of Anointing Revival and Leadership Explosion Event in one conference that catapults the saints into higher dimensions of leadership, breakthrough, freedom, influence and impact.

www.12slm.org
www.vision-fest.org

www.ingramcontent.com/pod-product-compliance
Lightning Source LLC
Chambersburg PA
CBHW080535030426
42337CB00023B/4746